Operation Breathe Easy

A child's lung transplant story

Story by Joan Powers
Illustrations by Michelle Caudle

Operation Breathe Easy

ISBN-10: 1519475071
ISBN-13: 978-1519475077

This book is dedicated to my friend Tom.

Today is an exciting but scary day for Tommy. He loves to ride his bike, play baseball and take hikes. He likes going to school. Mostly Tommy likes to help people.

Tommy had a cough and trouble catching his breath.
His mom took him to the pediatrician,
Dr. Button.

Dr. Button asked Tommy's mom to get some medicine at the store.
Tommy took it for a few days but it didn't help.

Dr. Button sent Tommy for some tests. The nurses were very nice.
They made sure he was comfortable when they took his x-rays and
drew his blood.

Tommy and his mom and dad went to Dr. Button's office to get the results. Dr. Button told them Tommy's lungs were sick. They didn't work right.

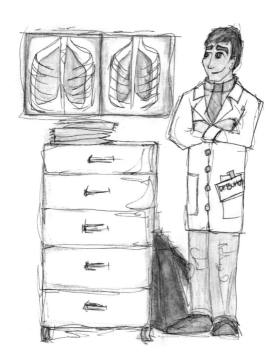

He said Tommy will need an operation, a lung transplant. During the operation Dr. Button will replace Tommy's sick lungs with healthy lungs.

Tommy's mom and dad read him books about transplants. The books helped answer his questions.
Tommy's healthy lungs will be donated by another person.
"*I guess someone else likes to help people, just like I do.*"
Tommy thought.
He knows that another family had to lose a special person for him to get his new lungs.
That makes him happy and sad.

While Tommy waited for his new lungs he wore a special mask to help him breathe.
The mask looks funny but it doesn't hurt and helps him to breathe easier.

Tommy got tired when he walked because his body had to work hard to breathe. His legs worked fine but he used a wheelchair to get around.

Today is the day Tommy has been waiting for his new lungs are ready. Tommy has been looking forward to this operation. After it is done and his body heals, he will play with his friends and go back to school.

Tommy uses his wheelchair most of the time. Today he asks if he can walk into the hospital. Mom and dad say okay but he must hold onto the railing. Tommy brings his teddy bear *Bart* to keep him company.
Tommy is very brave.

The doctors and nurses are waiting for Tommy when he gets to the hospital. They are all there to care for him. He has been to the hospital many times and already knows some of the doctors and nurses.

Dr. Button comes to say hello. Tommy likes Dr. Button. They tell each other *"knock knock"* jokes that make them both laugh. Tommy has seen Dr. Button many times. He still thinks it's funny for a doctor's last name to be "Button".

The doctor says it's time for Tommy to get his new lungs. Everyone has told Tommy that everything will be okay but now that the operation is here he feels scared.
His mom and dad say it's okay to be scared.

Tommy has his own special room in the hospital where he will stay for his entire visit. The machines in the room will help him feel better after his operation. Tommy has a big bed that can go up, down, and bend in the middle. Tommy will want to play with the buttons on the bed. There is one very important button he can push to call the nurse if he needs something.

Everyone who visits Tommy will need to wash their hands and put a mask and gown on before entering his room. Not just his mom and dad, but all of the doctors and nurses too!
This will help keep germs away from Tommy while he gets better.

It's time to go to the operating room. A nice nurse comes in and puts a soft, blue hat on Tommy's head to cover his hair. Tommy smiles when he thinks about his dog wearing a mask and gown.

The nurse rolls Tommy's bed to the operating room. Tommy's mom and dad will sit in a waiting room nearby. During the operation a nurse will come to the waiting room and let them know everything is okay.

The operating room has big lights. Everyone is busy getting ready. Tommy is there for a short time before he is given special medicine and falls asleep.

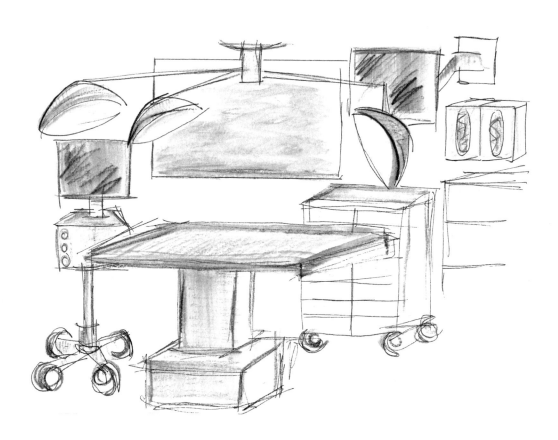

After his operation, Tommy opens his eyes and sees his mom and dad. He doesn't remember anything about it. Dr. Button says that is how it's supposed to be. Tommy has a cuff on his arm that gives a gentle squeeze once in a while. The tube he had in his mouth to help him breathe is now out. He only needs an oxygen mask like before the operation.

The nurses make sure he has warm blankets too. All of these things will help his body heal. Tommy wants to talk about his operation but for now he and his new lungs need to rest.

It will take a while for Tommy to feel better after his surgery.
Everyone is thinking of ways to help him
when he gets home.

Tommy's Nana is thinking about cooking his favorite foods. Eating
healthy foods will help Tommy to get strong.   Grandpa knows all of
Tommy's favorite books so he can read to him so he won't get bored.

Tommy tries hard to do everything the doctors and nurses tell him to do. He has been in the hospital for a few days and wants to go home. Dr. Button comes in daily to check on Tommy. Today, he tells Tommy that he is doing great and tomorrow he can get out of bed and take a short walk in the hallway.
No wheelchair and no oxygen mask!

Everyone is happy to hear Tommy is doing well. His friends made him get well cards. His mom hangs them in his hospital room.

The nurses and doctors tell Tommy they have never seen so many cards! Some are very funny. They make Tommy happy.

Tommy gets stronger every day. He is breathing easier and does not get as tired. Tommy hears that some other children at the hospital need transplant operations. Ethan needs a kidney, Rachel a liver and Fiona a heart.

Tommy has an idea!

He wants to tell the other children his story about being sick and how the transplant operation made him feel better! By talking with the children, he could make it less scary by letting them know what to expect.

Dr. Button thinks Tommy's idea is wonderful. He goes with Tommy to see the children. Tommy tells his story. Tommy says all kids are different so each of them will have a different story to tell after they have their transplant operation. The children are so happy to hear Tommy's story.

Tommy used to think he was the only kid who had to have a transplant operation. Now he has a lot of friends who have had a transplant.

Before Tommy got sick, he had a lot of energy and enjoyed helping people. He can't wait to help his neighbor, Mr. Smalley, take his trash barrels to the curb on trash day. He looks forward to helping Mrs. Walker with her cat Twinkle Toes. Once, Twinkle Toes was stuck in a tree and Tommy climbed up and rescued her. He can't wait to climb trees again.

Today is a special day. Tommy can finally go home. He is going to miss the nurses who took such good care of him and the doctors who would come in every day to make sure he was healing. However, he is excited about sleeping in his own bed at night with his dog.

When Tommy gets home, Mr. Smalley, Mrs. Walker and Twinkle Toes are outside waiting for him. They wave hello. They have missed Tommy and are glad to see him.

Tommy is glad to see his neighbors and gives them a big wave before he kneels down and gives his dog a big hug.

The ride home made Tommy sleepy. He crawls into his bed, takes a long, deep breath with his new lungs and falls asleep. He feels almost like he did before he got sick. Tommy will have to take it easy until he gets all of his strength back.

Tomorrow he will visit with his friends. Tonight he dreams about playing baseball, taking hikes and going to school like he used to.

29429301R00020

Made in the USA
Middletown, DE
18 February 2016